Our planet
Workbook 2

Earth in space
- Earth, sun and moon ... 2
- The planets ... 4
- Day and night ... 6
- Land and water ... 8

Planet Earth
- A living planet ... 10
- The shape of the land ... 12
- Volcanoes ... 14
- World wonders ... 16

Weather and seasons
- Experiencing the weather ... 18
- Different types of weather ... 20
- Extreme weather ... 22
- The seasons ... 24
- Going round the sun ... 26

Local areas
- Shelter ... 28
- Houses around the world ... 30
- Living in a village ... 32
- Exploring local streets ... 34
- Under your feet ... 36

Maps and plans
- Maps and stories ... 38
- Treasure island ... 40
- Different plans ... 42
- The view from above ... 44

The United Kingdom
- Countries and capitals in the United Kingdom ... 46
- Mountains, rivers and seas in the United Kingdom ... 48

Different environments
- Living in the Arctic ... 50
- Living in the rainforest ... 52
- Living in the desert ... 54
- Animals around the world ... 56

World maps
- World continents and oceans ... 58
- World countries ... 60

Fiona Macgregor

Earth, sun and moon

1. Label the picture of the Earth and the sun.
2. Try and look for the moon this week. What shape is it? Draw a picture of the moon in the box.
3. Which is the hottest: the Earth, sun or moon? Colour it in orange.

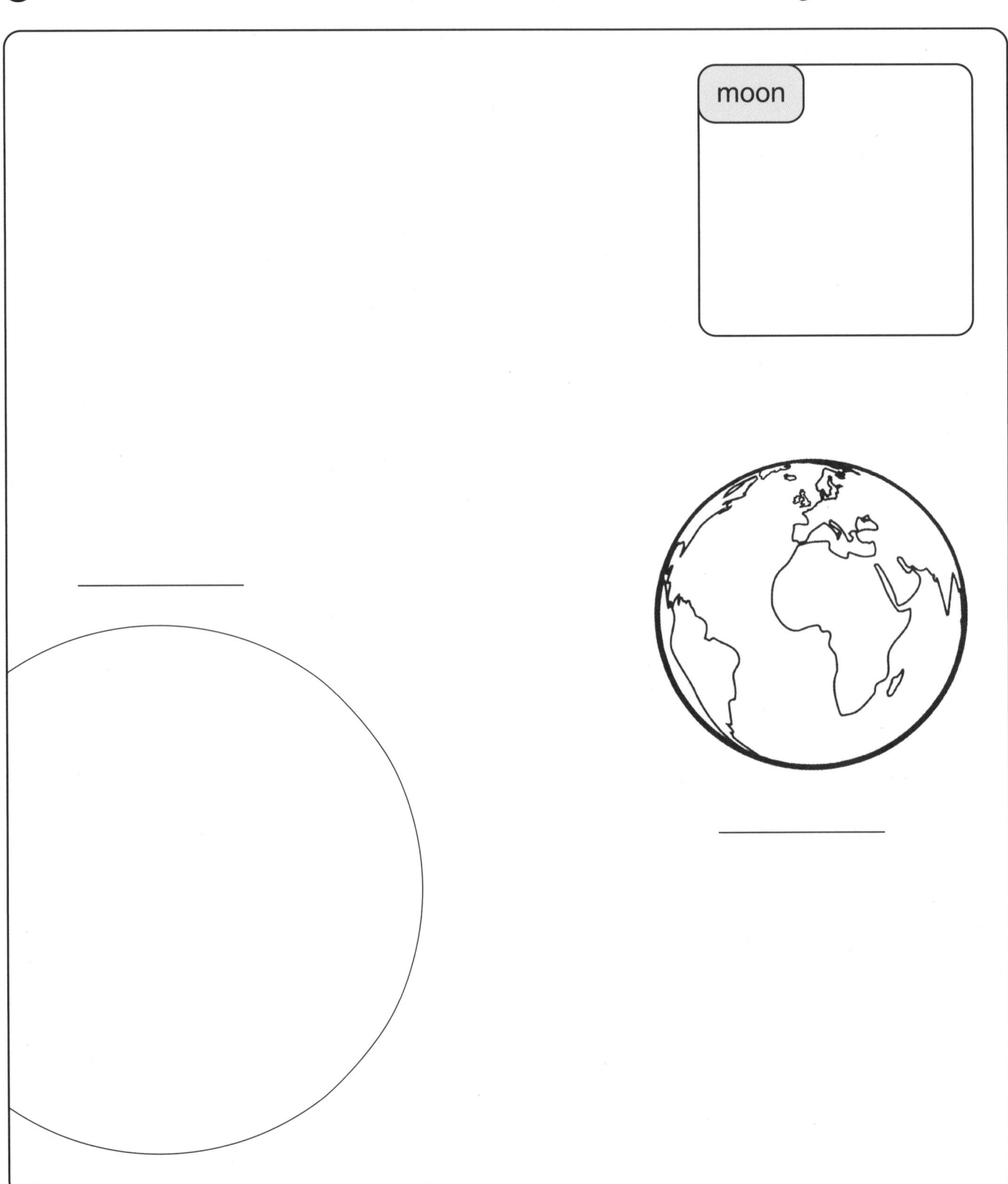

❹ Match a label to each picture. Write A or B in the corner.

Label A: The moon goes around the Earth.

Label B: The Earth goes around the sun.

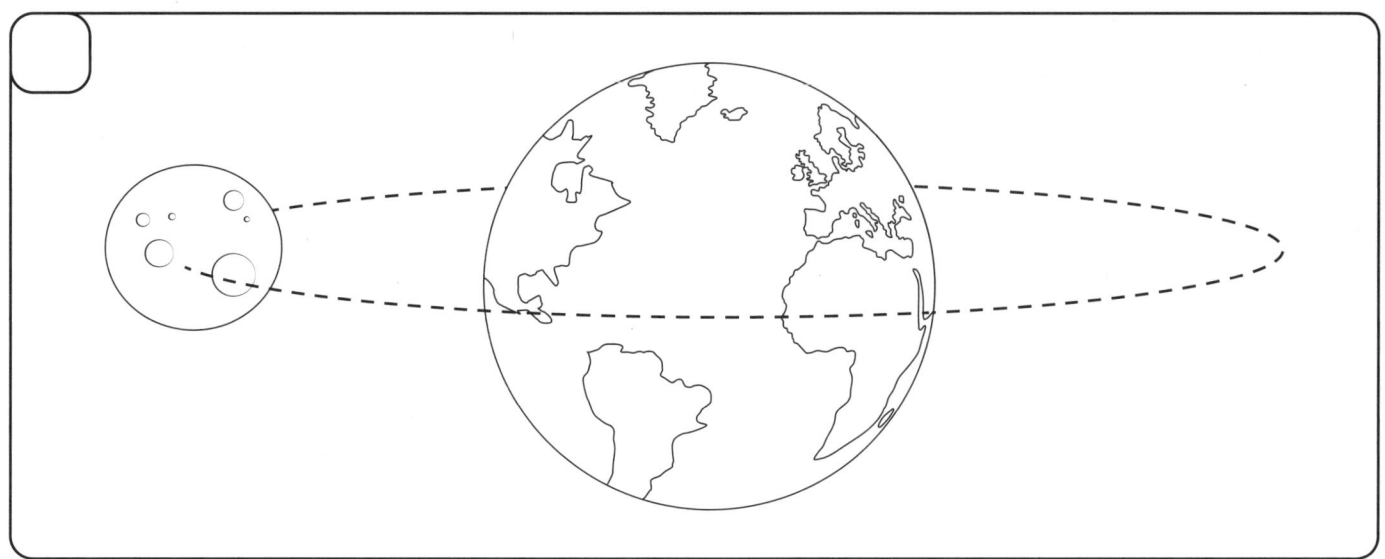

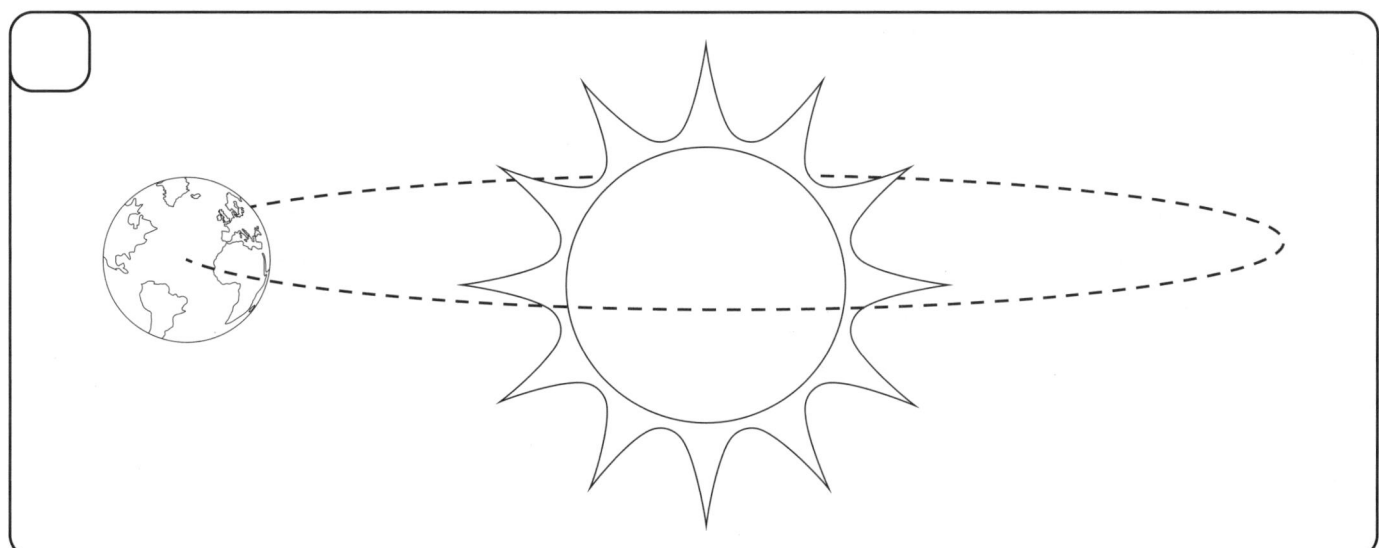

❺ True or false? Colour the answer.

a) The Earth goes around the moon.   True   **False**

b) The Earth goes around the sun.   True   False

c) The moon goes around the Earth.   True   False

d) The Earth is bigger than the sun.   True   False

e) The sun is bigger than the Earth.   True   False

3

The planets

❶ Label the picture using the words from the boxes below.

a) Label the planet that is **closest** to the sun.

b) Label the planet that is **furthest away** from the sun.

c) Label the planet **we live on**.

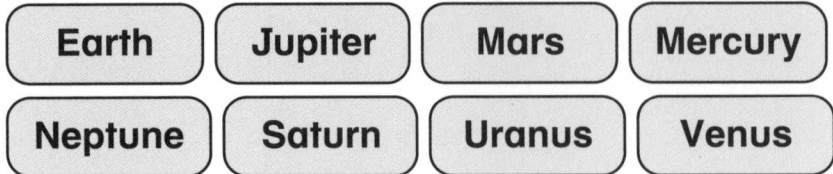

Earth	Jupiter	Mars	Mercury
Neptune	Saturn	Uranus	Venus

❷ Colour the planets in the picture.

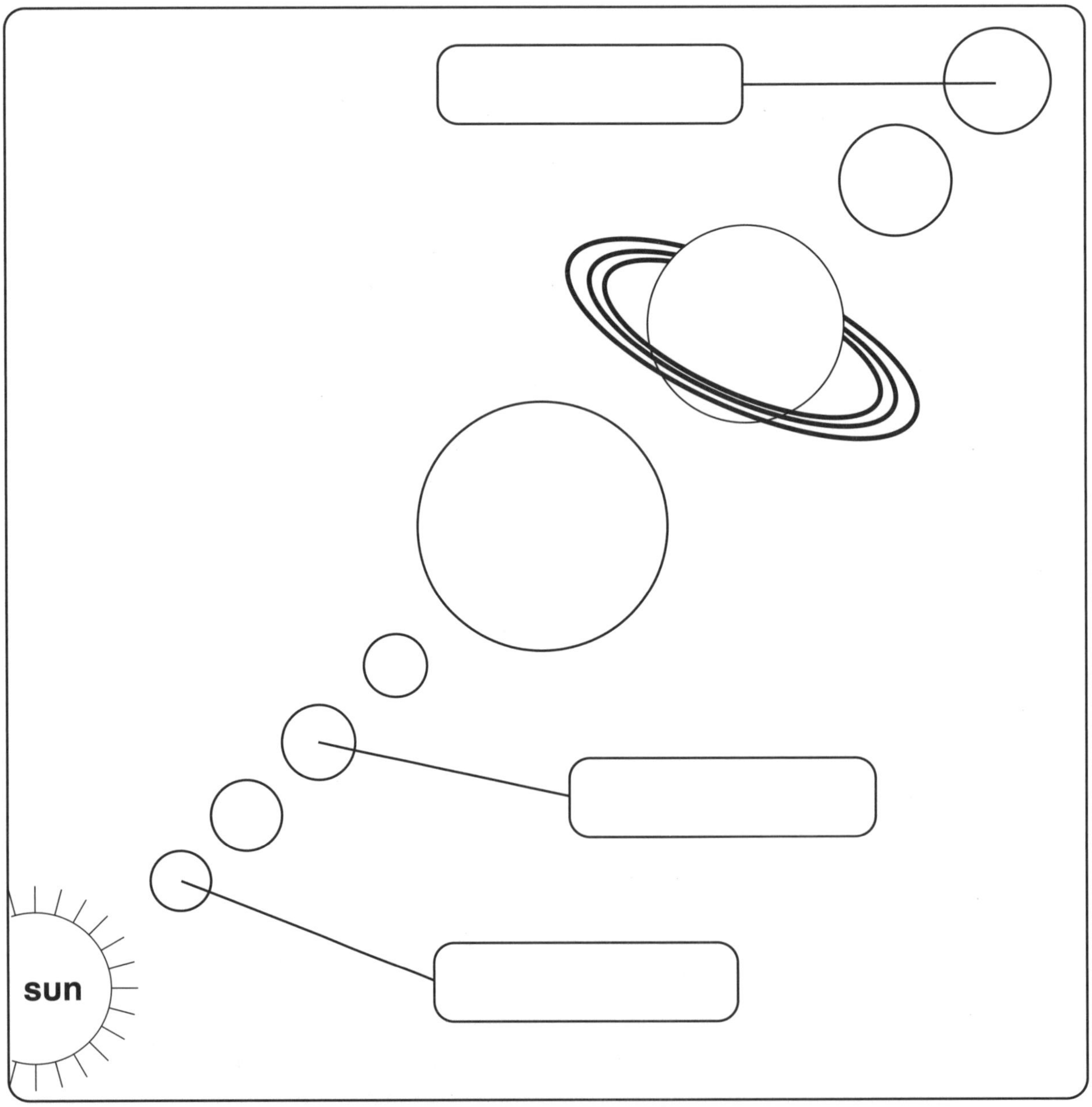

Hint: Look at pages 6 and 7 of your Pupil Book if you need help.

❸ Which two planets are next to Earth?

_____

_____

❹ Remember the order of the planets with a silly sentence!
Try making a silly sentence of your own.
Then draw a picture of your sentence.

My	M _____	Mercury
Very	V _____	Venus
Excellent	E _____	Earth
Mother	M _____	Mars
Just	J _____	Jupiter
Served	S _____	Saturn
Us	U _____	Uranus
Noodles.	N _____	Neptune

5

Day and night

1 Use a coloured pencil to follow the path the moon makes around the Earth.

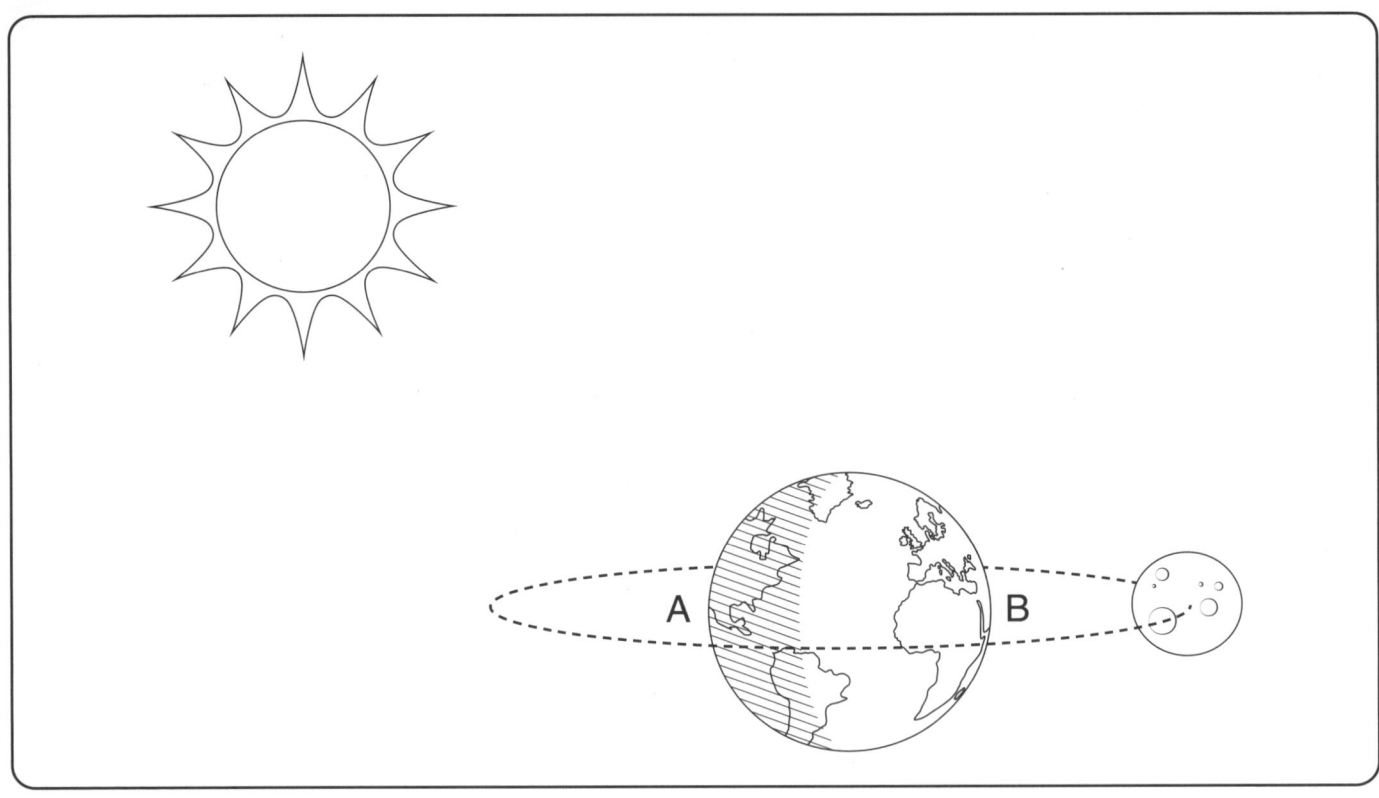

2 Look at the picture of the moon's path around the Earth.

    a) Which side of the Earth is daytime: A or B? _____

    b) Which side of the Earth is night-time: A or B? _____

3 Draw or stick in a picture of an animal that is awake at night-time.

❹ Look at this picture of the Earth. Label the picture using the words in the boxes.

| North Pole | South Pole | equator |

Hint: Look at page 8 of your Pupil Book if you need help.

Land and water

❶ Use a coloured pencil to follow Max as he tunnels down into the Earth.

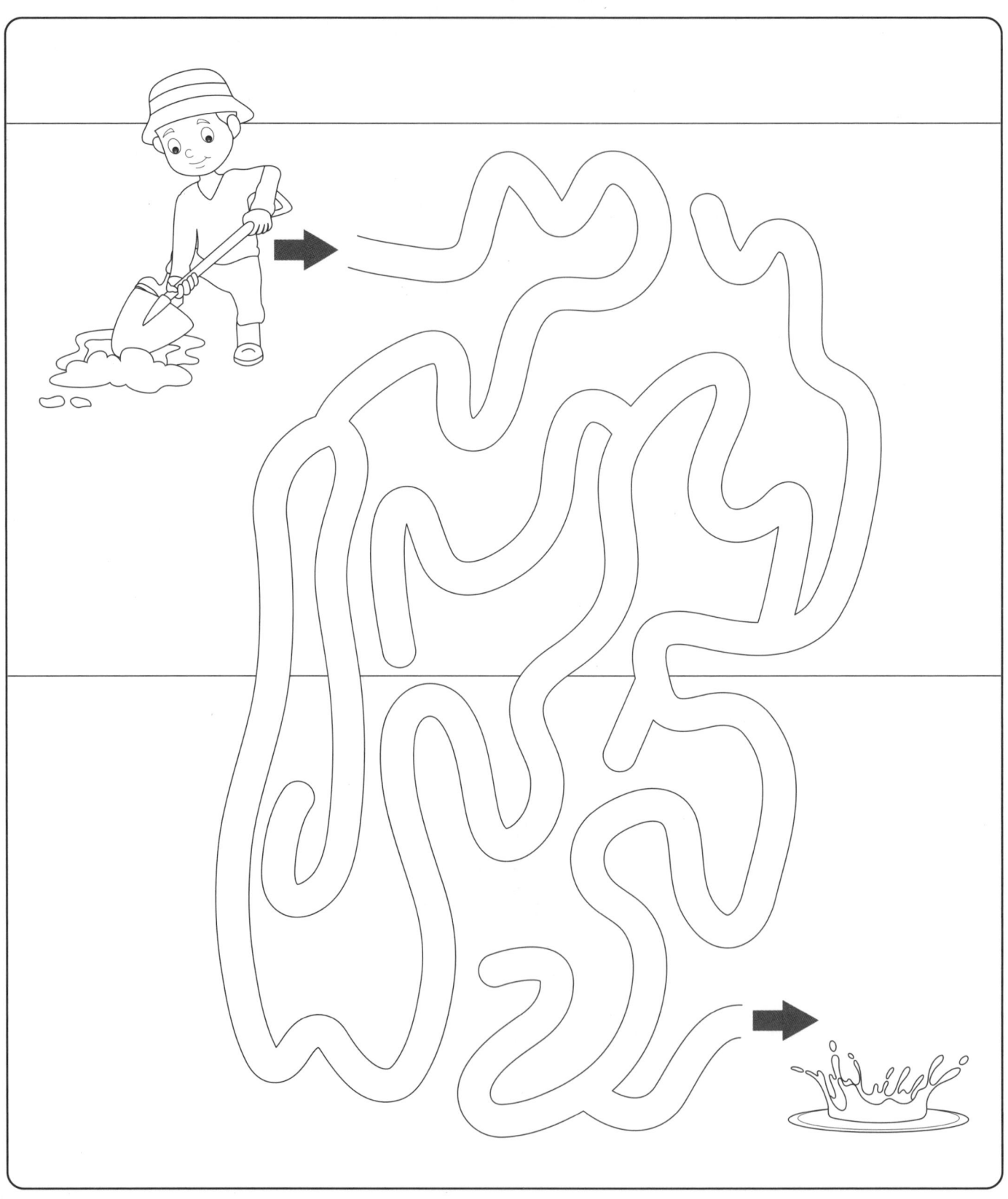

❷ Write what you think Max will find on his way down the tunnel.

_____

3 Look at the picture on page 11 of your Pupil Book.

a) Is there more land or more water on Earth? Colour the answer.

more land | **more water**

b) Do you think you can drink the seawater? Explain why or why not.

____

____

4 a) Label the picture using the words from the boxes below.

lake | **sea** | **river** | **ocean**

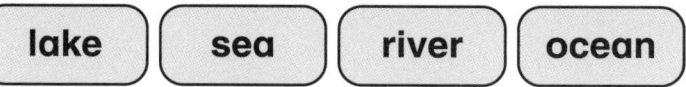

b) Colour all of the water in blue.

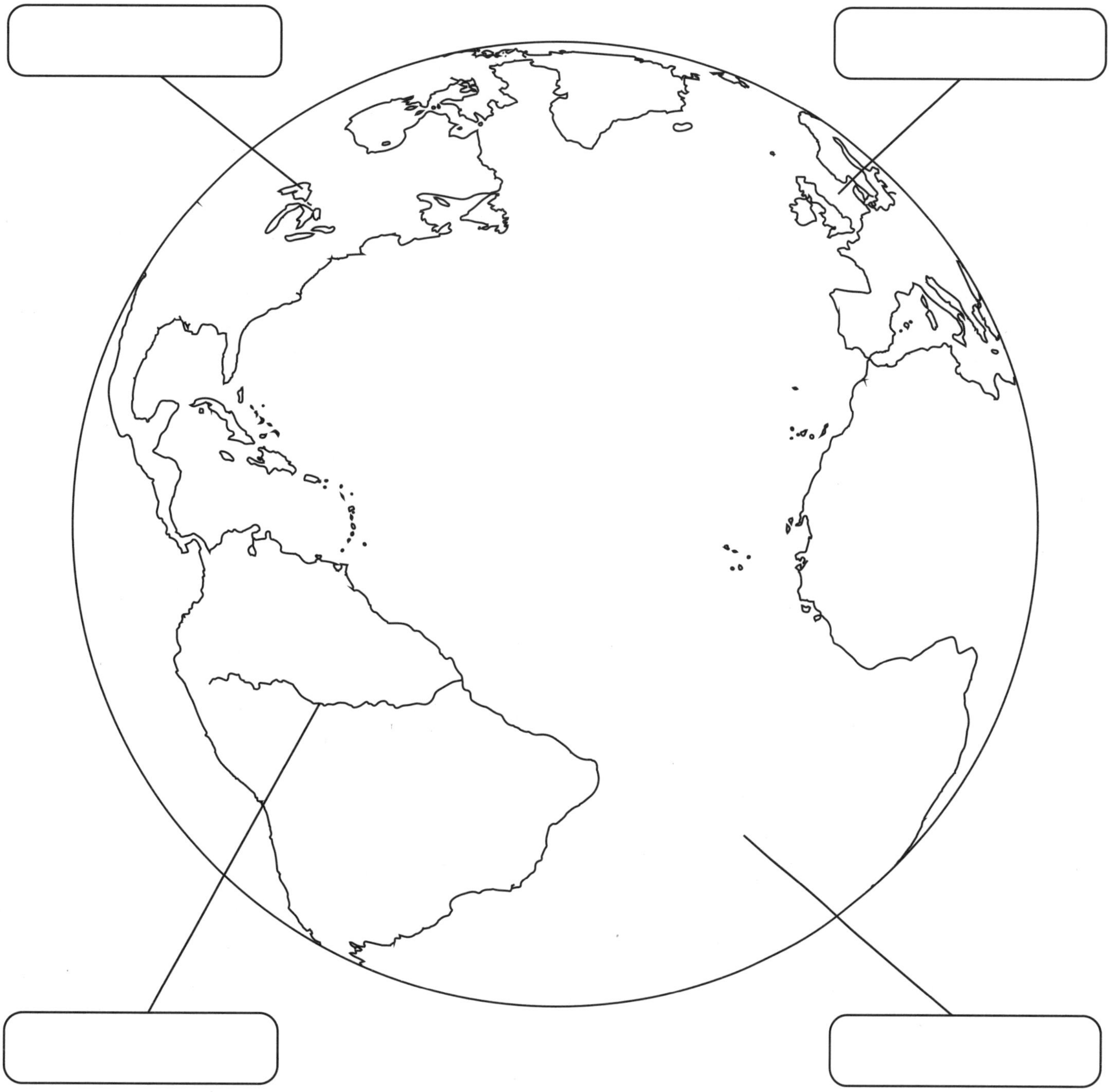

A living planet

1 What do plants need to grow? Draw lines to match the labels to the pictures.

air   soil   sun   water

2 Look at the pictures of the tomato plant as it grows.

   a) Colour in the pictures.

   b) Label the pictures using the words from the boxes below.

   roots   stem   leaves   flowers   seed

3 Look at these two animals that live in different water habitats.

otter

fish

Why is water important for these animals? Write one sentence for each picture.

_____

_____

Hint: Do fish drink water?

4 Why is water important in your life?

_____

11

The shape of the land

❶ Colour the river on its journey from the mountains to the sea.

❷ Look at the picture. Write five things that the river passes on its journey to the sea.

1 _____   4 _____

2 _____   5 _____

3 _____

3 Test your landscape vocabulary.

Circle these words hidden in the puzzle.

| mountain | pool | current | valley | cliff |
| river | downstream | waterfall | sea |

h	c	u	r	r	e	n	t	g	m
w	a	t	e	r	f	a	l	l	o
p	b	v	v	l	f	r	w	m	u
o	z	k	a	c	l	i	f	f	n
o	h	p	l	v	y	r	c	s	t
l	u	d	l	i	o	i	z	y	a
x	m	w	e	t	g	v	n	s	i
e	q	k	y	q	j	e	a	e	n
d	o	w	n	s	t	r	e	a	m

4 Choose one of the words from Activity 3. Draw a picture and write a sentence about it.

13

Volcanoes

1 Think about what happens when a volcano erupts.

a) Colour in the key.

b) Use the key to colour the volcano.

Key

hot melted rocks	red
gas	black

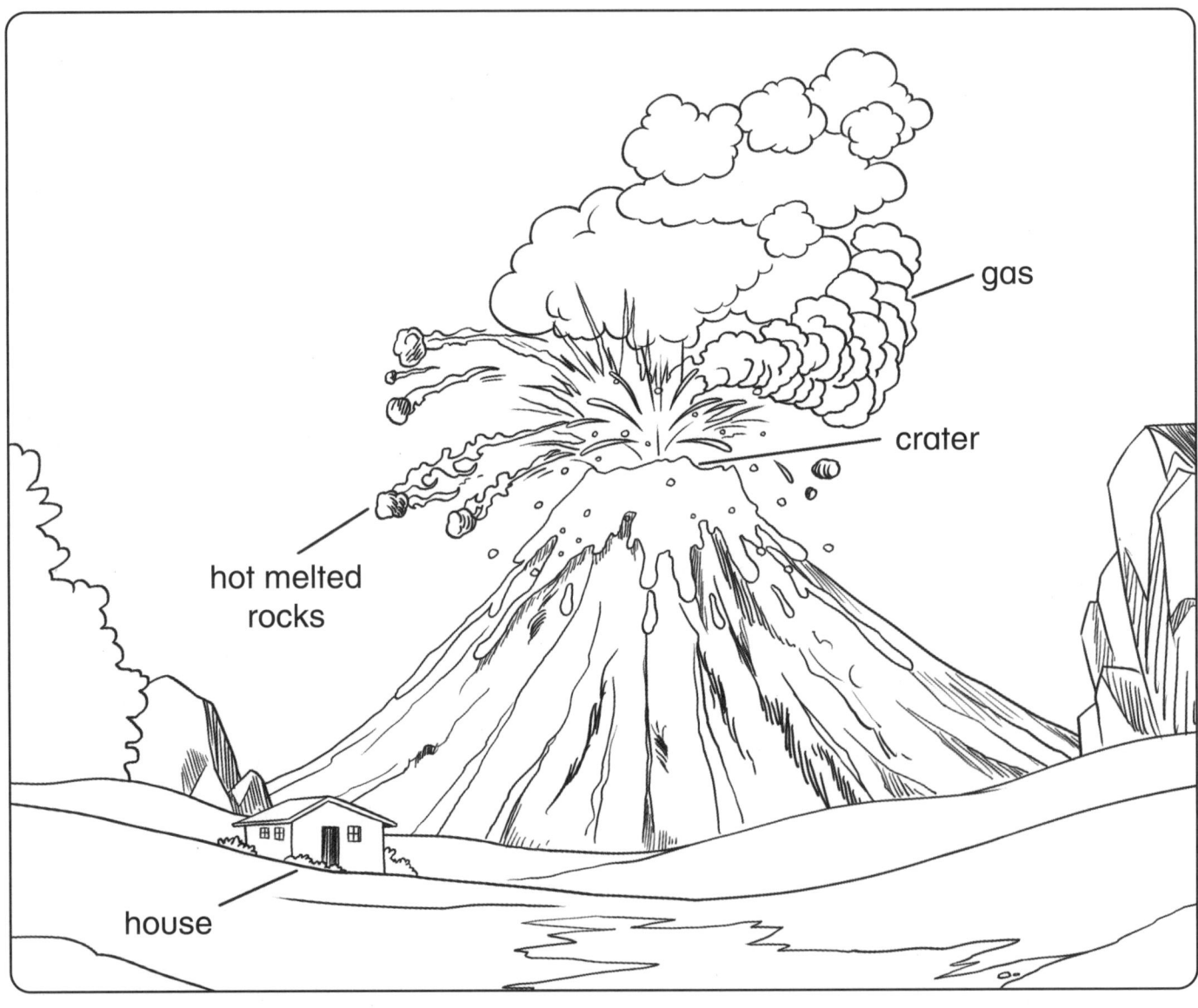

2 Read the story on page 16 of your Pupil Book. What would you tell Azim to do if he heard rumbling sounds coming from the volcano? Write two good pieces of advice.

_____

_____

3 Write your own story about a volcano.

Use the words from the boxes in your story.

Give your story an exciting title.

| volcano | erupt | gas | hot rocks |

World wonders

1 Look at page 18 of your Pupil Book.

    a) Draw the three wonders of the world that Azim saw.

    b) Write labels for each picture in the small boxes.

2 There are many wonders in our world. Here are two more of them.

    Draw a line to match the caption to the correct picture.

The Great Barrier Reef in Australia is one of the longest reefs in the world, with amazing sea life.

Stonehenge in the UK is a mystery! Who put all those huge boulders in a circle? How did they do it?

❸ What is a special sight in your country?

   a) Draw a picture or stick in a photograph of the special sight in the middle box.

   b) Write its name below the picture.

   c) Write four facts about what makes it special in the boxes around the picture.

Name:

Experiencing the weather

1 Colour in the pictures. Use warm colours for the warm, dry day and cool colours for the cold, wet day.

Hint: Look at a colour wheel to find warm colours and cool colours.

A warm, dry day

A cold, wet day

18

❷ Draw pictures to show these weather words.

hot cold wet windy

❸ Colour in the pictures. Use warm colours for warm weather and cool colours for cold weather.

Different types of weather

❶ Read the story on page 22 of your Pupil Book. This is Mika. Add clothes to the picture, so that Mika is dressed correctly when the weather changes in the story.

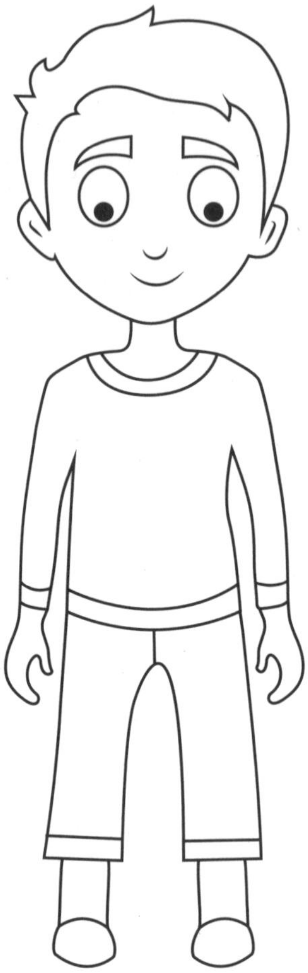

❷ What will Mika find useful? Circle the useful items.

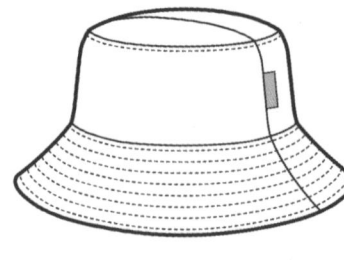

❸ Choose four types of weather. Draw your own weather symbols in each box. Write a label for each drawing.

_____	_____	_____	_____

❹ Record the weather for a week at school. Draw symbols in each box.

Monday	
Tuesday	
Wednesday	
Thursday	
Friday	

Hint: Does the weather always stay the same all day? You can draw more than one symbol in each box.

Extreme weather

1 Label the pictures using the words from the boxes below.

   hurricane   tornado   flood   sandstorm

2 Colour the pictures.

3 What weather emergency might close your school?

   a) Draw a picture in the space below.

   b) Write sentences to show what your picture shows.

My picture shows:

_____

_____

_____

_____

The seasons

❶ Look at the symbols in the boxes. Write the name of each season on the lines below.

❷ Write the months that make up each season in your country.

Season: _____

Which months of the year is this season where you live?

_____

_____

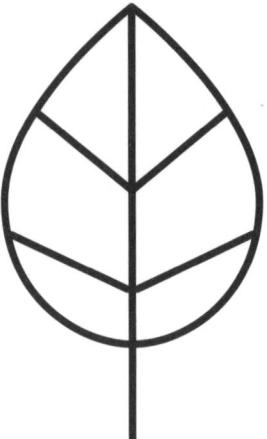

Season: _____

Which months of the year is this season where you live?

_____

_____

Season: _____

Which months of the year is this season where you live?

_____

_____

Season: _____

Which months of the year is this season where you live?

_____

_____

❸ What do you like doing at different times in the year?

   a) Draw something that you like to do in June, September, December and March.

   b) Write a sentence about each of your drawings.

   c) Draw a weather symbol in the small box to show what the weather is like in that month where you live.

In June I like to _____.

In September I like to _____.

In December I like to _____.

In March I like to _____.

Going round the sun

1 Finish the sentences using the best words from the boxes.

summer   winter

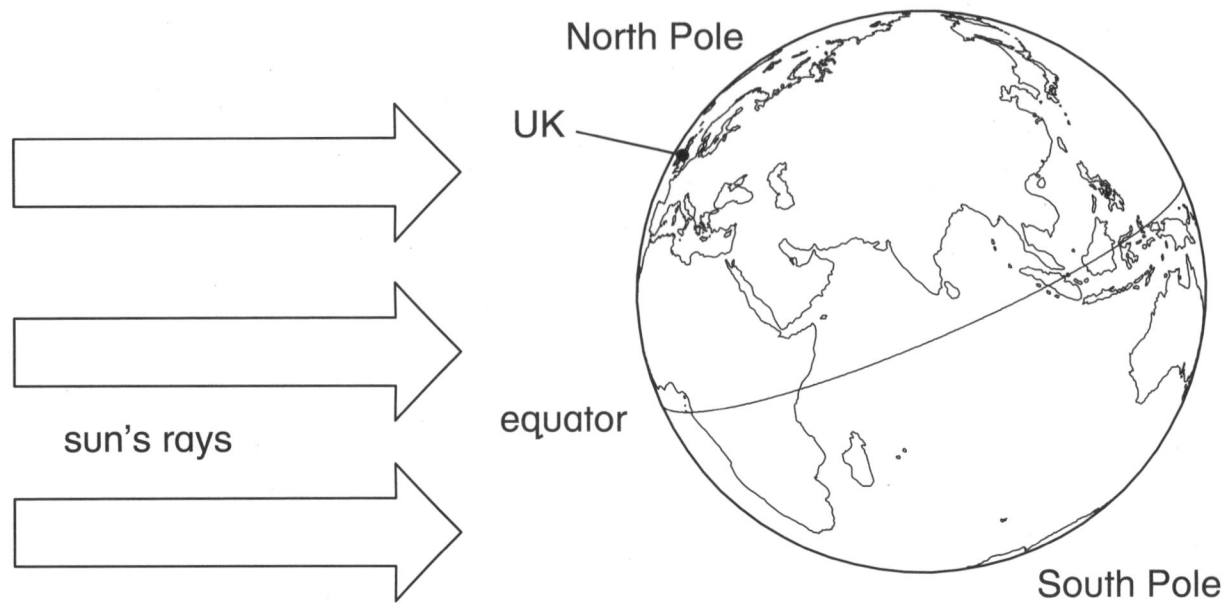

It is _____ in the United Kingdom in this picture.

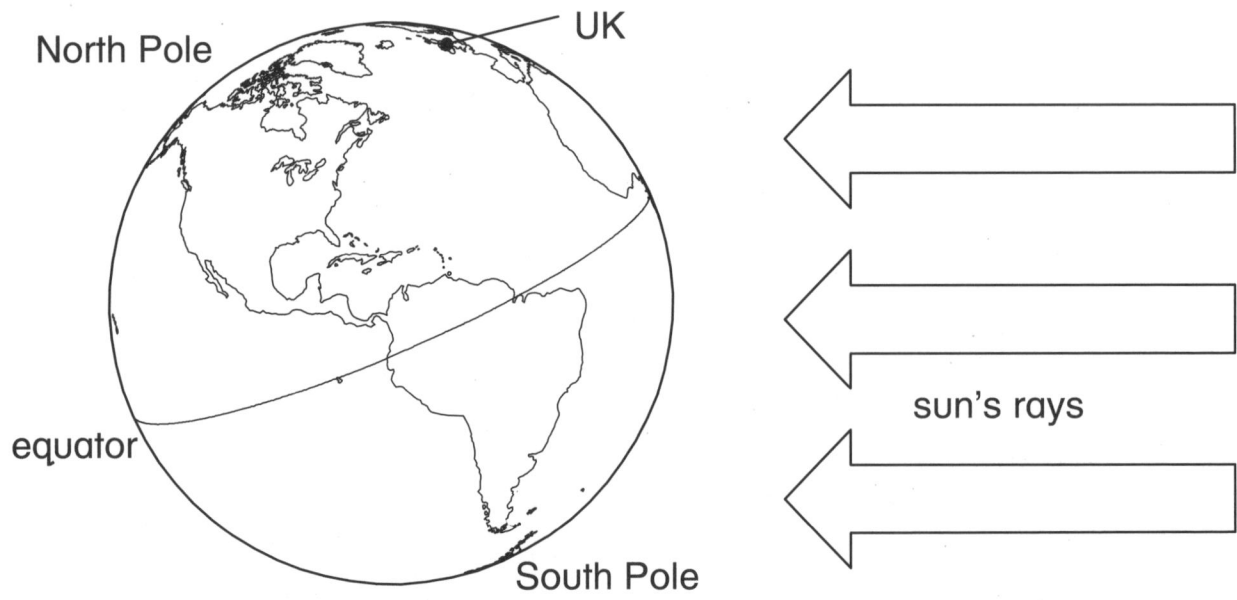

It is _____ in the United Kingdom in this picture.

26

2 Test your weather words.

Complete this crossword puzzle.

Across
1. The year is divided into four s_____.
2. The sun is out in the day and the _____ is out at night.
3. There is a North and a South _____.
4. Water falling from the sky is called _____.
5. When it is blowy outside, we say the weather is w_____.

Down
6. In this season, the weather is hot: _____.
7. The Earth goes around the _____.
8. In winter in the United Kingdom, the weather is c_____.
9. In winter, the United Kingdom tilts _____ from the sun.
10. The opposite of the South Pole is the _____ Pole.

Shelter

1 Make a list of some reasons we need a shelter or a house.

_____   _____

_____   _____

2 What are the differences between a house and a tent? Add your ideas to the table.

House	Tent

3 Have you ever been camping? Did you like staying in a tent?

Write about why you liked it or why you did not like it.

Use your answers from Activity 2 to help you.

If you haven't been camping, imagine what you would and wouldn't like about it.

_____

_____

_____

4 Make a plan to build a model house, using recycled materials.

Look at the example in the picture. You can use any of the materials shown in the boxes below. You may use other materials too.

Draw your model in the box. Label the materials you will use.

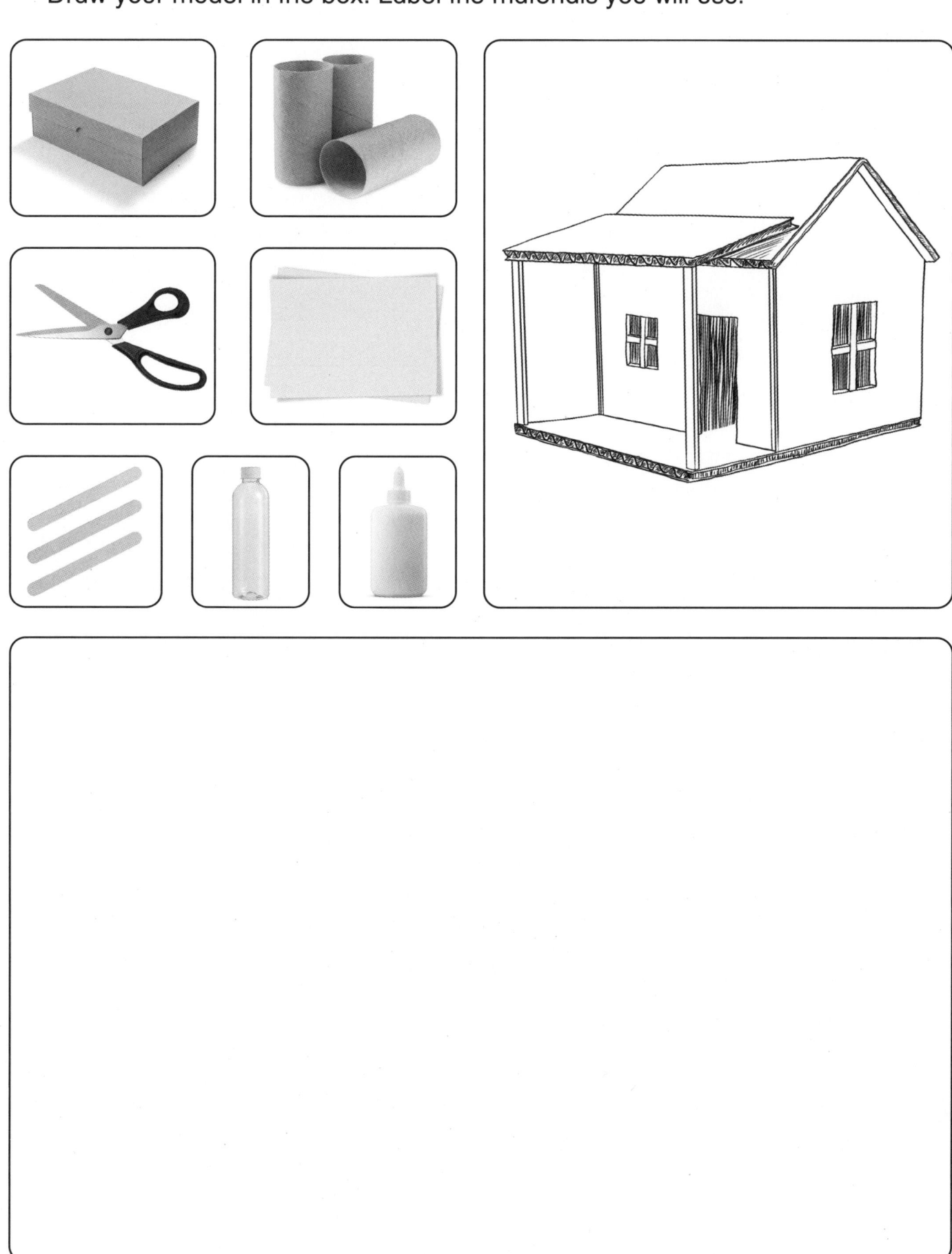

Houses around the world

❶ What are these houses made of? Write the best word under the pictures.

bricks   wood   stone   metal   glass

_____

_____

_____

_____

_____

❷ Circle the type of home you would most like to live in.
Why did you choose that house? Write a sentence.

_____

_____

30

3 Draw a sketch of your house.

4 What is your house made of? Use the list of materials in the boxes on page 30 to help you.

_____

_____

5 Write your address.

_____

_____

_____

_____

Living in a village

❶ Finish the drawing of the village. Draw the missing places in the boxes.

❷ Draw a route you could take if you were walking:

a) from the farm to the garage

b) from the school to the football pitch.

Hint: Use a different colour for each route.

❸ On page 29, you planned a model house. In this activity, you will plan a village. Do your planning here.

Your village needs:
- a field where people can gather
- homes for people to live
- a shop for basic supplies
- a garage or petrol station
- roads, with stop signs where the roads meet.

Your class may decide to make the model houses you planned earlier and other buildings, then put them together to form a village.

Exploring local streets

1 Write the labels under the correct pictures of the street furniture.

post boxes   metal manhole covers   drains   fire hydrants

shop signs   overhead wires   advertisements   bus stops

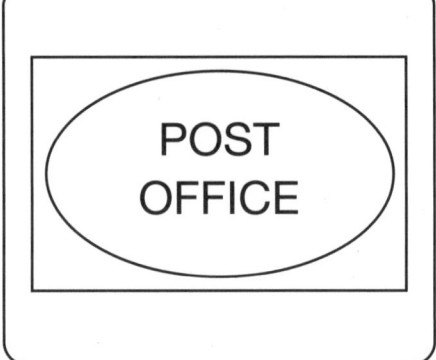

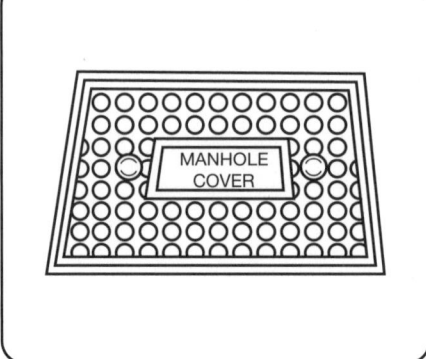

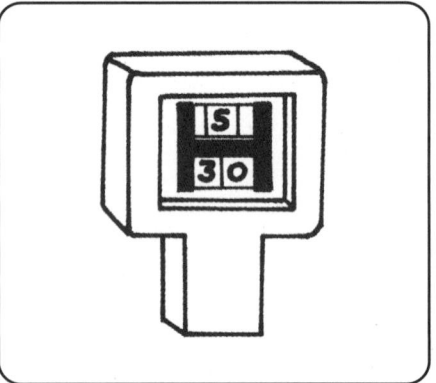

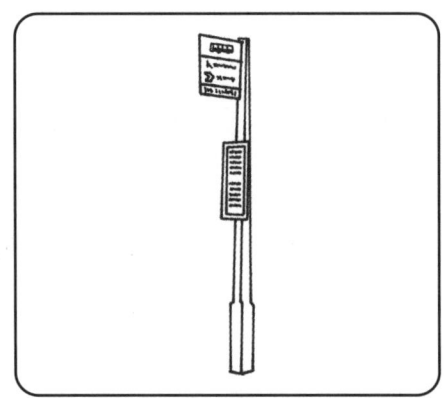

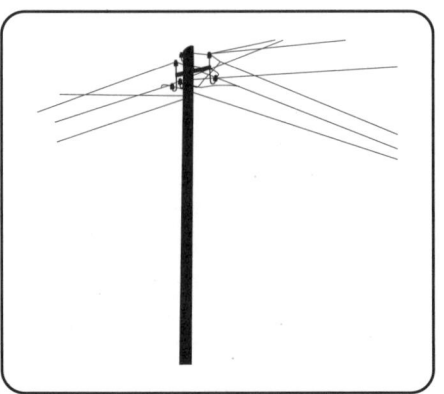

2 Draw pictures or take photographs of different street furniture near your school or your home.

> **Hint:** Use the list in Activity 1 to help you.
>
> Some other things you might find include pavements, litter bins, benches and trees.

3 Stick your photographs or drawings here.

   a) Write a label for each drawing.

   b) Write how many of each thing you found, e.g. five trees, one bench.

Under your feet

❶ Which of these lines go:

a) into a house, and

b) out of a house?

Label the lines on the drawing.

| clean water | wastewater | electricity | rainwater | gas |

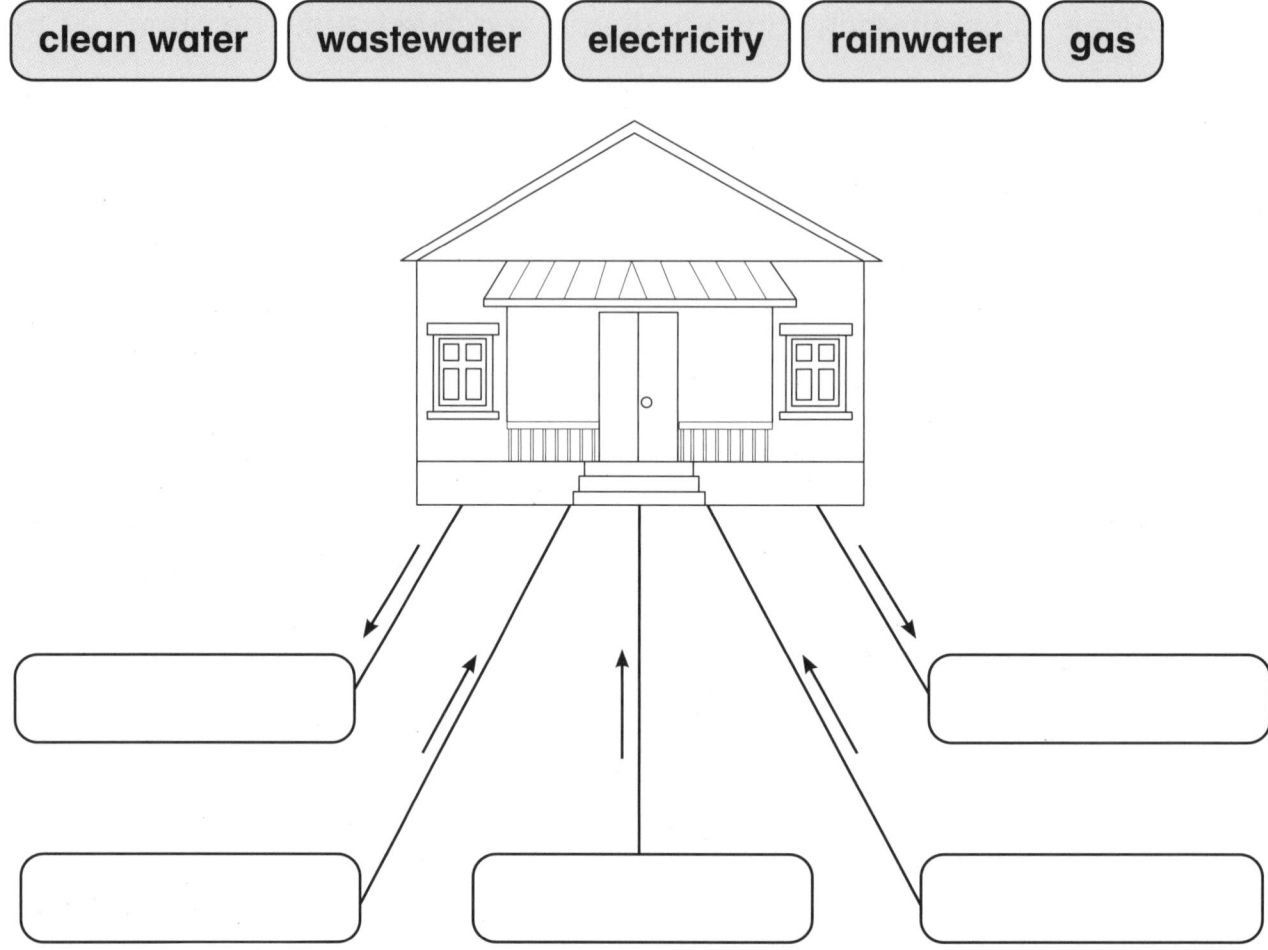

❷ Which of these is carried in a pipe and which in a cable?

Colour the correct answer.

clean water   pipe   cable

wastewater   pipe   cable

electricity   pipe   cable

rainwater   pipe   cable

gas   pipe   cable

❸ Test your local area vocabulary.

Find these words in the wordsearch.

street	underground	flats
drain	village	homes
field	air	shelter
pipe	farm	bins

v	i	l	l	a	g	e	j	z	x	q
e	h	s	f	s	h	e	l	t	e	r
s	o	p	i	p	e	f	f	a	r	m
t	m	o	e	b	d	l	m	d	v	p
r	e	w	l	n	g	a	k	r	l	y
e	s	j	d	y	x	t	z	a	k	j
e	r	z	f	q	u	s	b	i	n	s
t	x	a	i	r	v	z	h	n	w	a
u	n	d	e	r	g	r	o	u	n	d

❹ Choose one of the words from Activity 3 and use it in a sentence to show you know what it means.

_____

_____

37

Maps and stories

1 Read the story on page 40 of your Pupil Book. How many places did the hare and the tortoise pass on their way to the lettuces? Make a list.

_____

_____

_____

2 Draw a journey map of the story of the hare and the tortoise.

3 Draw a picture map of your favourite story.

4 Ask an older person about what it was like to grow up in the place where you live. Write three interesting things that they tell you.

_____

_____

_____

Treasure island

1 Look at the map on page 43 of the Pupil Book. Write the grid squares for:

a) the lighthouse _____A1_____

b) the windmill _____

c) the mountains _____

d) the castle _____

e) the sailing boat in the bay _____

f) the farm _____

g) the north forest _____

> **Hint:** When you give a grid reference, remember to use the right order. This may help you to remember: Along the hall **(A)**, and up the stairs **(1)**.

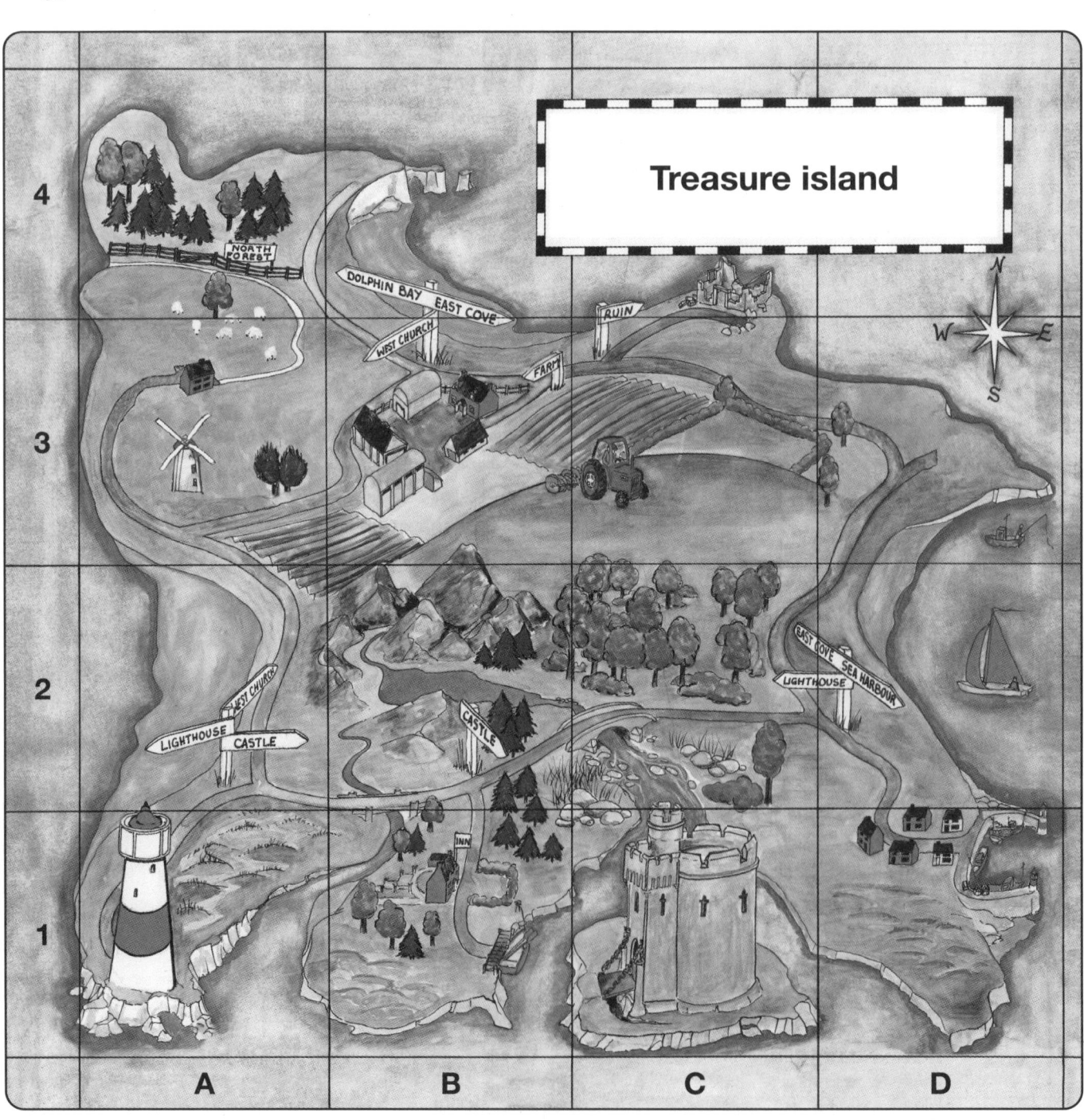

❷ Think about your way home from somewhere you often visit – maybe from school or a friend's house. Make a note of:
- the things you pass on the way
- where you walk on roads or paths
- where you turn or cross the road.

_____

_____

_____

❸ Draw a map of your route home.
   a) Label the different places on your route.
   b) Draw small pictures to show the places you pass.

Different plans

1 Draw lines to match each picture to the right plan.

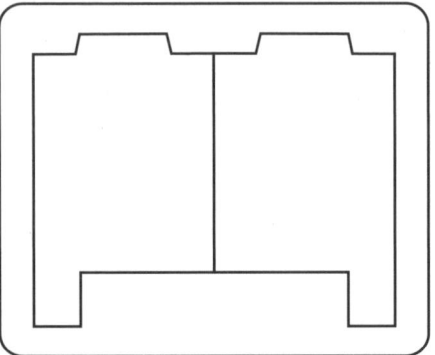 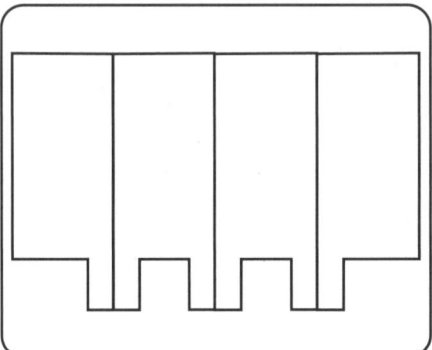 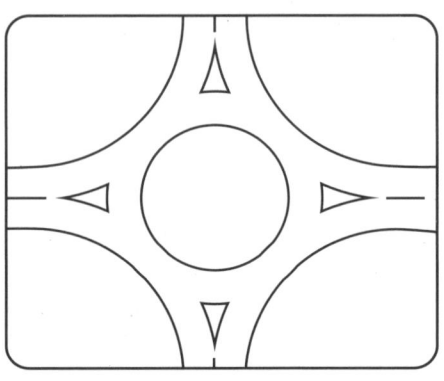

2 What is the shape of your classroom? Look at this example.

What do you think all the shapes represent? Label them.

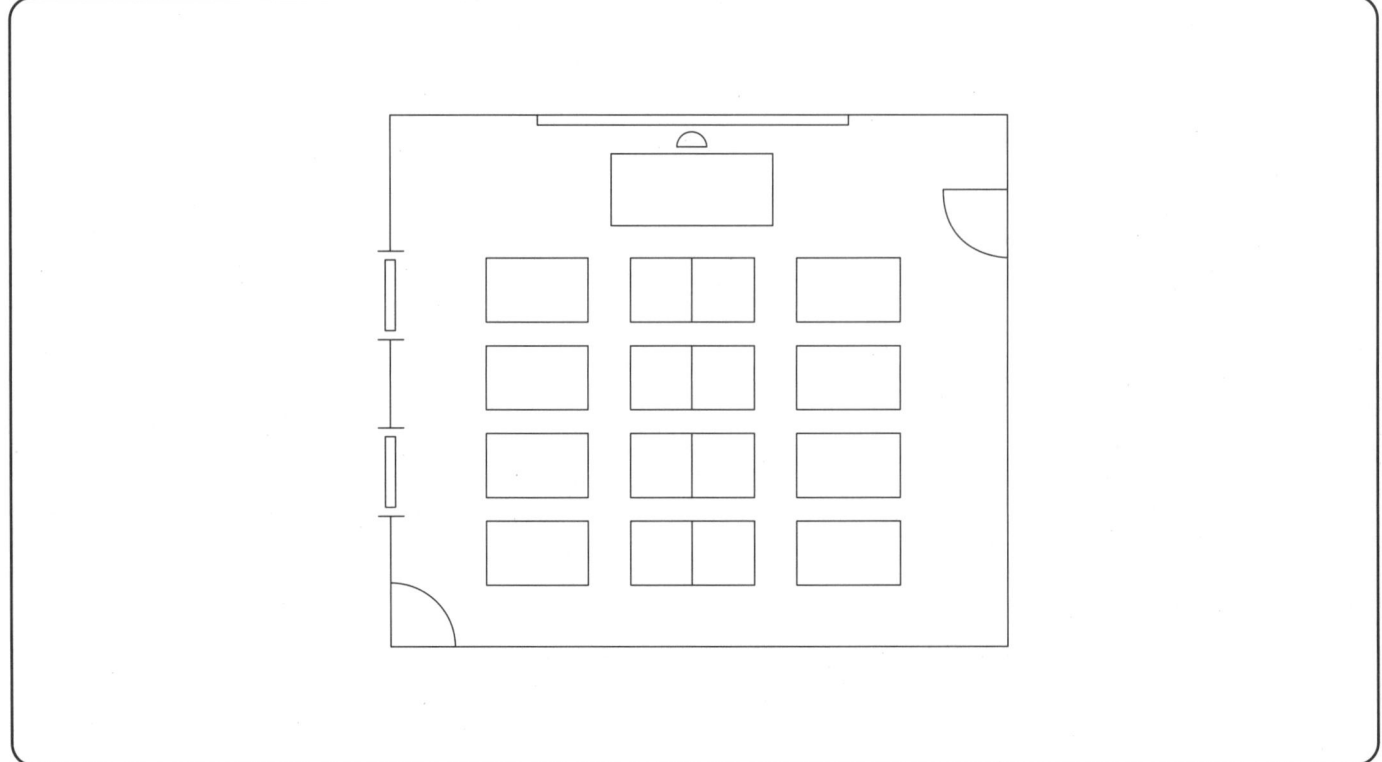

3 Draw a floor plan of your classroom.

   a) Use small squares, rectangles or circles to show the tables.

   b) Remember to put in doors and windows.

   c) Label the different features of your classroom.

The view from above

1 What things can you see in this picture? Match the places to their grid references on the lines below.

sheep pen | bridge | mountains | tractor | barn | lake

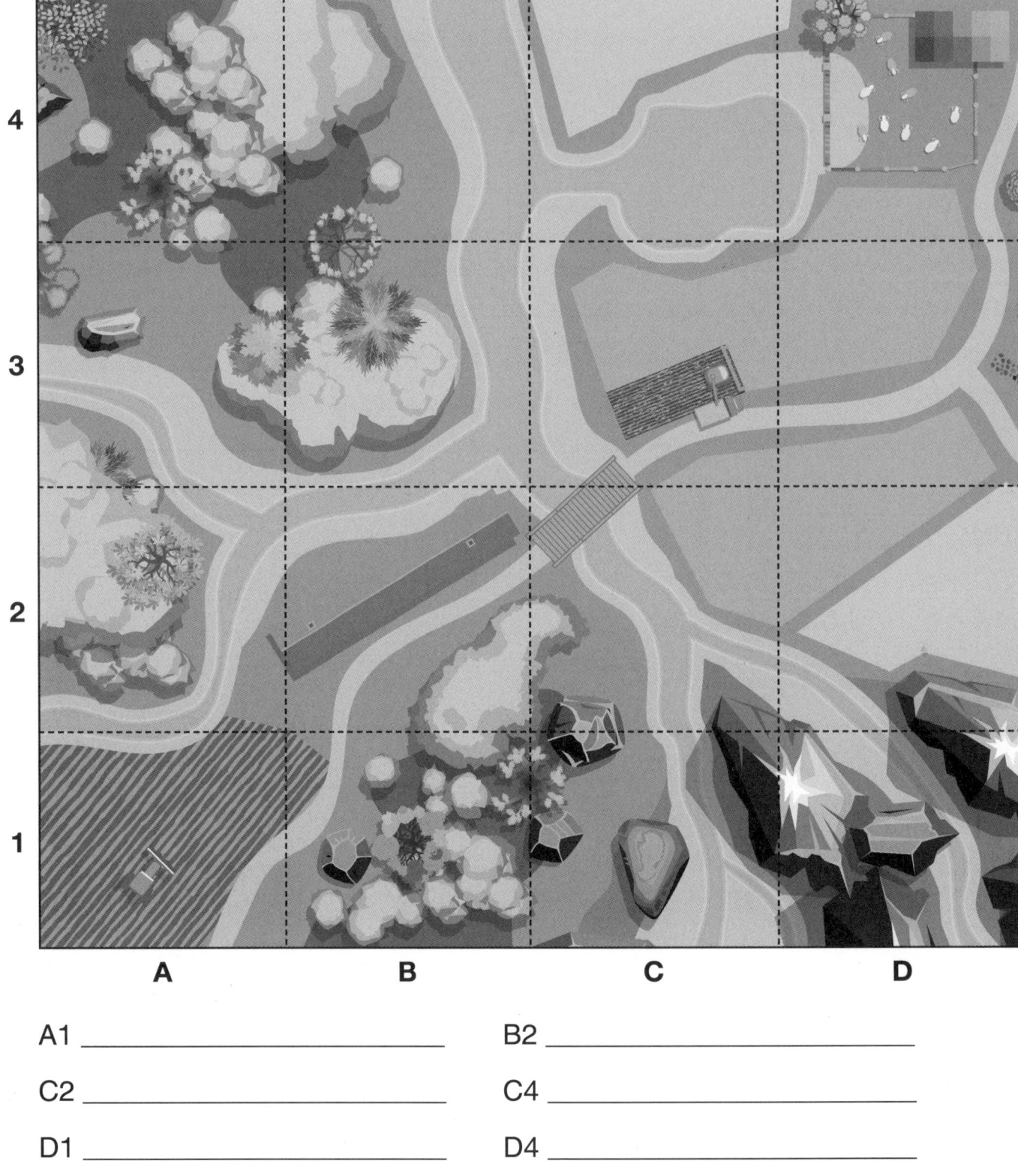

A1 _____ B2 _____

C2 _____ C4 _____

D1 _____ D4 _____

2 Look at this house, viewed from above. It is as if someone has taken the roof off.

   a) Name the rooms you can see.

   _____

   _____

   b) Write a list of the furniture you can see.

   _____

   _____

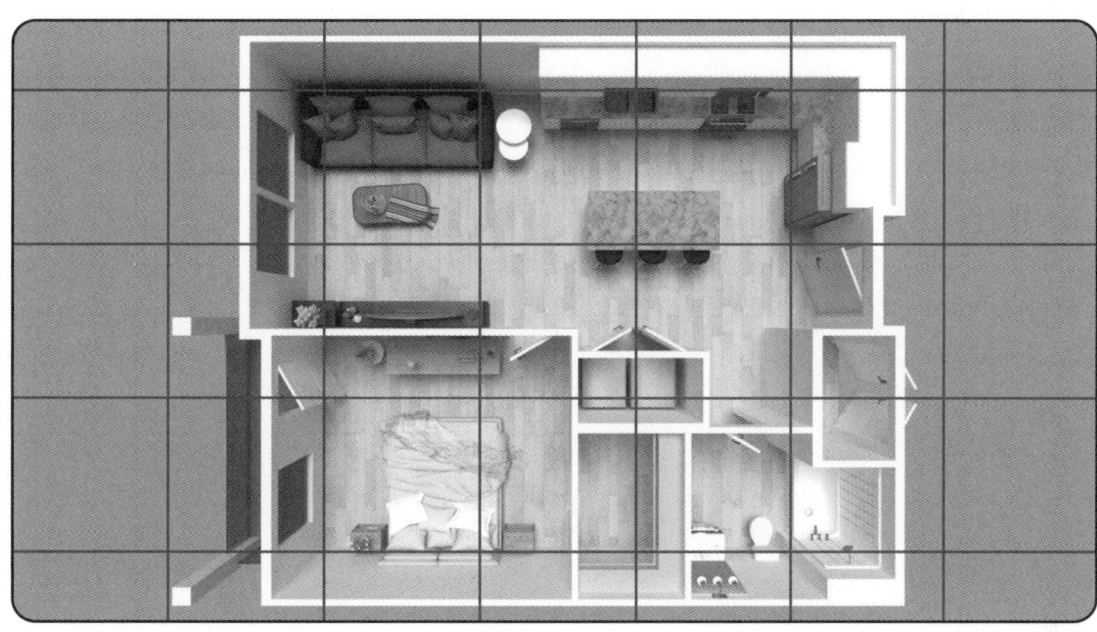

3 Draw a plan of the house, as seen from above. You can use a grid square to help you.

45

Countries and capitals in the United Kingdom

1 Each of the countries in the United Kingdom has its own flag. Find out the colours of the flag of Wales and colour it in.

Hint: Look in an atlas or research online.

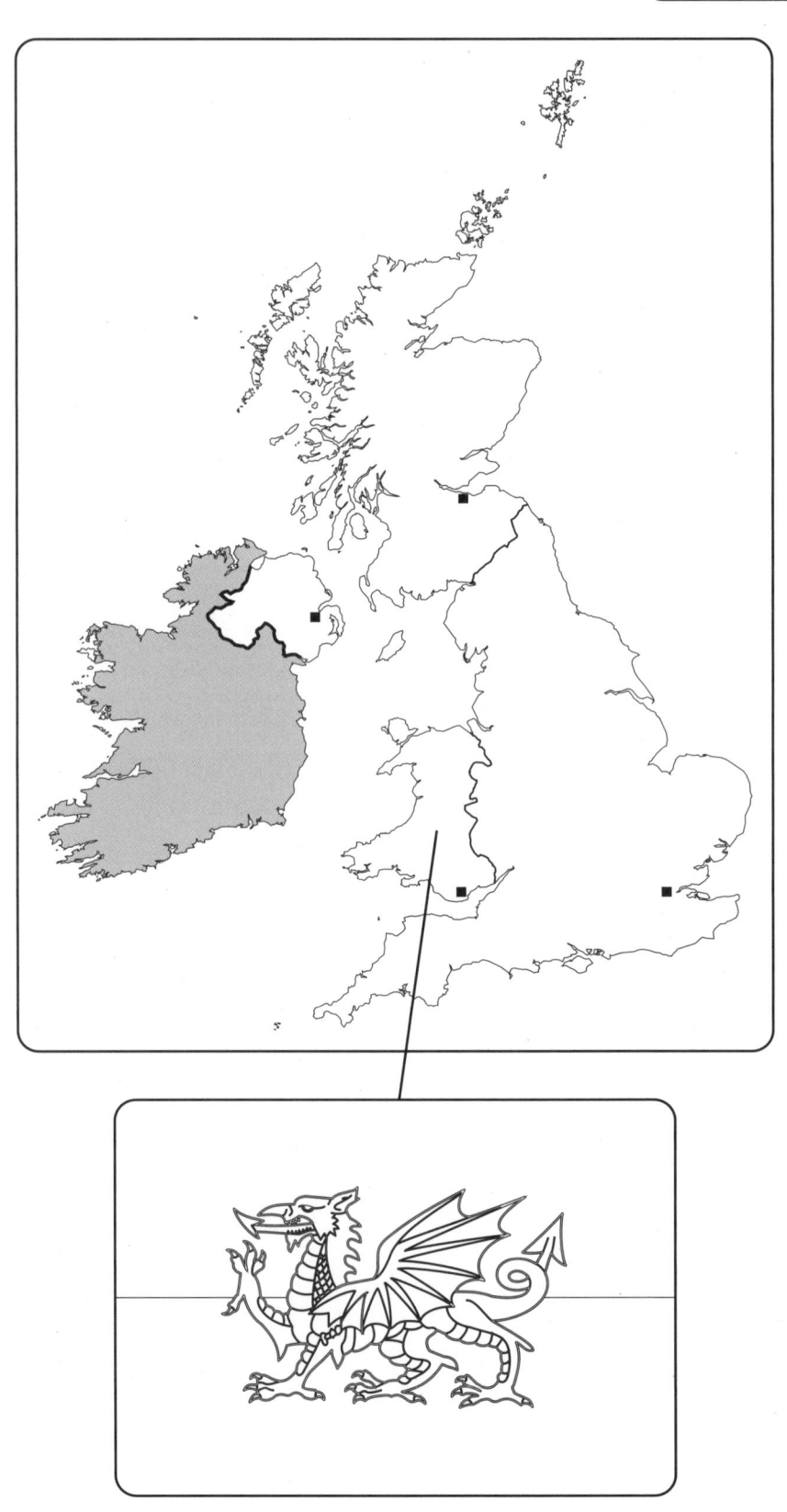

2 Find out more about one of the countries in the United Kingdom that you would like to visit. Make a fact file.

   a) Write three interesting facts about the country.

   b) Stick in a photograph or draw a picture to add to your research. Give your picture a caption.

Fact file

Country: _____

Capital city: _____

Fact 1: _____

Fact 2: _____

Fact 3: _____

What the picture shows: _____

Mountains, rivers and seas in the United Kingdom

❶ On the map, colour:
   a) the mountains green
   b) the rivers blue.

❷ Finish the labels to name some of the mountains and rivers in the United Kingdom.

Hint: Look at the map on page 51 of your Pupil Book if you need help with the names.

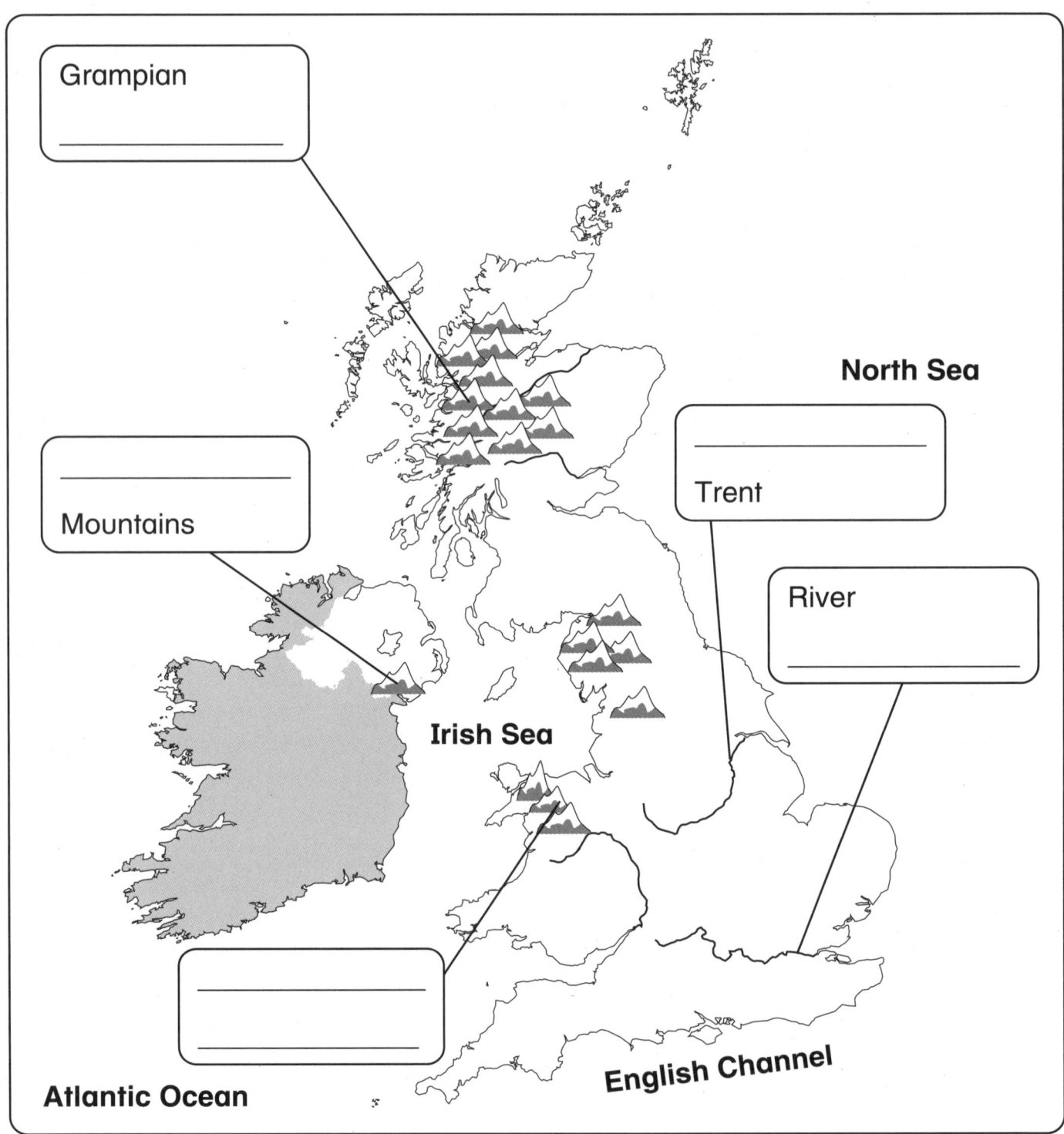

3 a) Use pages 48 to 51 of your Pupil Book to write five interesting questions about the United Kingdom. Leave space for the answers.

   b) Swap your book with a friend and answer each other's questions.

Question 1

_____

Answer

_____

Question 2

_____

Answer

_____

Question 3

_____

Answer

_____

Question 4

_____

Answer

_____

Question 5

_____

Answer

_____

Living in the Arctic

❶ Look at the pictures.

   a) Colour the animals.

   b) ⓒircle the animals that live in the Arctic.

❷ What will happen to Arctic animals if too much of the ice in the Arctic melts? Write two ideas.

_____

_____

3 Choose one of these animals.

| polar bear | walrus | reindeer | Arctic fox |

Find out more about the animal.

a) Write a short paragraph, giving three interesting facts about the animal. Say:
- what they eat
- where they live
- how they survive in the cold.

_____
_____
_____
_____
_____
_____

b) Draw a picture of the animal or stick a photograph of it here.

Living in the rainforest

1 Look at the picture carefully.

a) Find and circle these animals in the picture.

parrot   jaguar   monkey   penguin   tiger

elephant   tortoise   peacock   snake

b) One of the animals does not belong in the rainforest. Write its name and say where it does belong.

The animal that does not belong: _____

Where it belongs: _____

2 Choose one of these animals.

| parrot | jaguar | hummingbird | anteater | butterfly |

Find out more about the animal.

a) Write a short paragraph, giving three interesting facts about the animal. Say:
- what they eat
- where they live
- how they survive in the rainforest.

_____

_____

_____

_____

_____

_____

b) Draw a picture of the animal or stick a photograph of it here.

53

Living in the desert

1 Most deserts are hot and dry. Find the correct path to help the camel find the waterhole.

2 Find out two interesting facts about how camels live in the heat. Write them down.

Fact 1:

_____

_____

Fact 2:

_____

_____

❸ Here is Mika again. Last time you dressed him for cold, wet weather.

This time, dress him for a trip to the desert.

Hint: Think about…
- shade
- protection from the heat
- water.

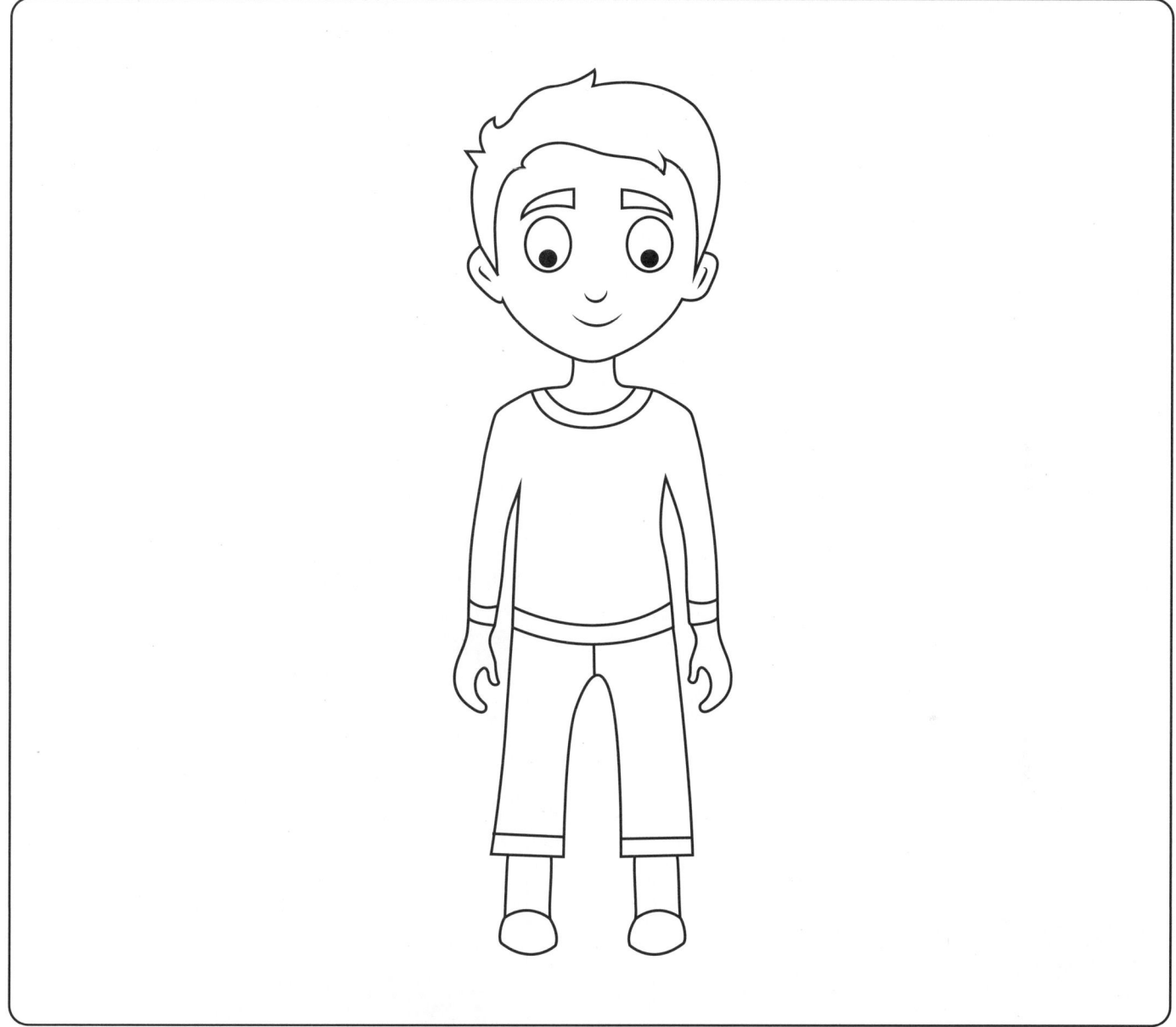

❹ Write a list of important things that Mika should take with him into the desert.

_____

_____

_____

_____

_____

55

Animals around the world

1 Draw a symbol for each of these habitats.

forests	deserts	polar lands	other lands

2 Write the names of the animals.

3 What sorts of lands do the animals live in? Draw your symbols next to each animal.

Hint: Look at pages 58 and 59 of your Pupil Book.

_____ _____

_____ _____

_____ _____

4 Write which continent each of the animals lives on.

> **Hint:** You can see the continents on pages 60 and 61 of your Pupil Book.

Polar bear _____

Panda _____

Tiger _____

King penguin _____

Amazon butterfly _____

Rocky Mountains eagle _____

5 Draw your favourite animal. Write a sentence about where it lives.

_____

_____

World continents and oceans

1 Write the names of the continents on the map.

Africa   Antarctica   Asia   Europe

North America   South America   Oceania

ARCTIC

ATLANTIC OCEAN

PACIFIC OCEAN

❷ Which continent do you live on? _____

❸ Colour your continent on the map. Use your favourite colour.

Hint: Look at pages 60 and 61 of your Pupil Book.

World countries

1. Label these countries on the map.

United States | Brazil | United Kingdom

Nigeria | China | Australia

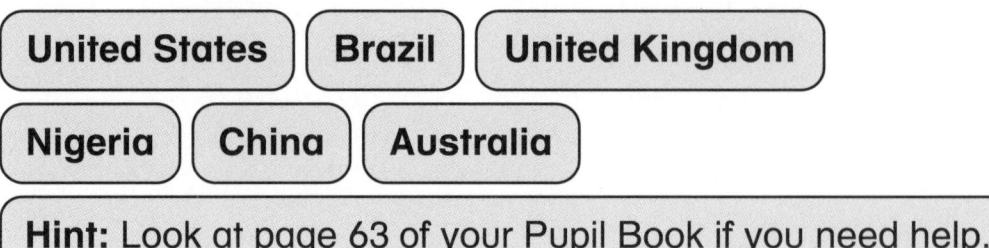

Hint: Look at page 63 of your Pupil Book if you need help.

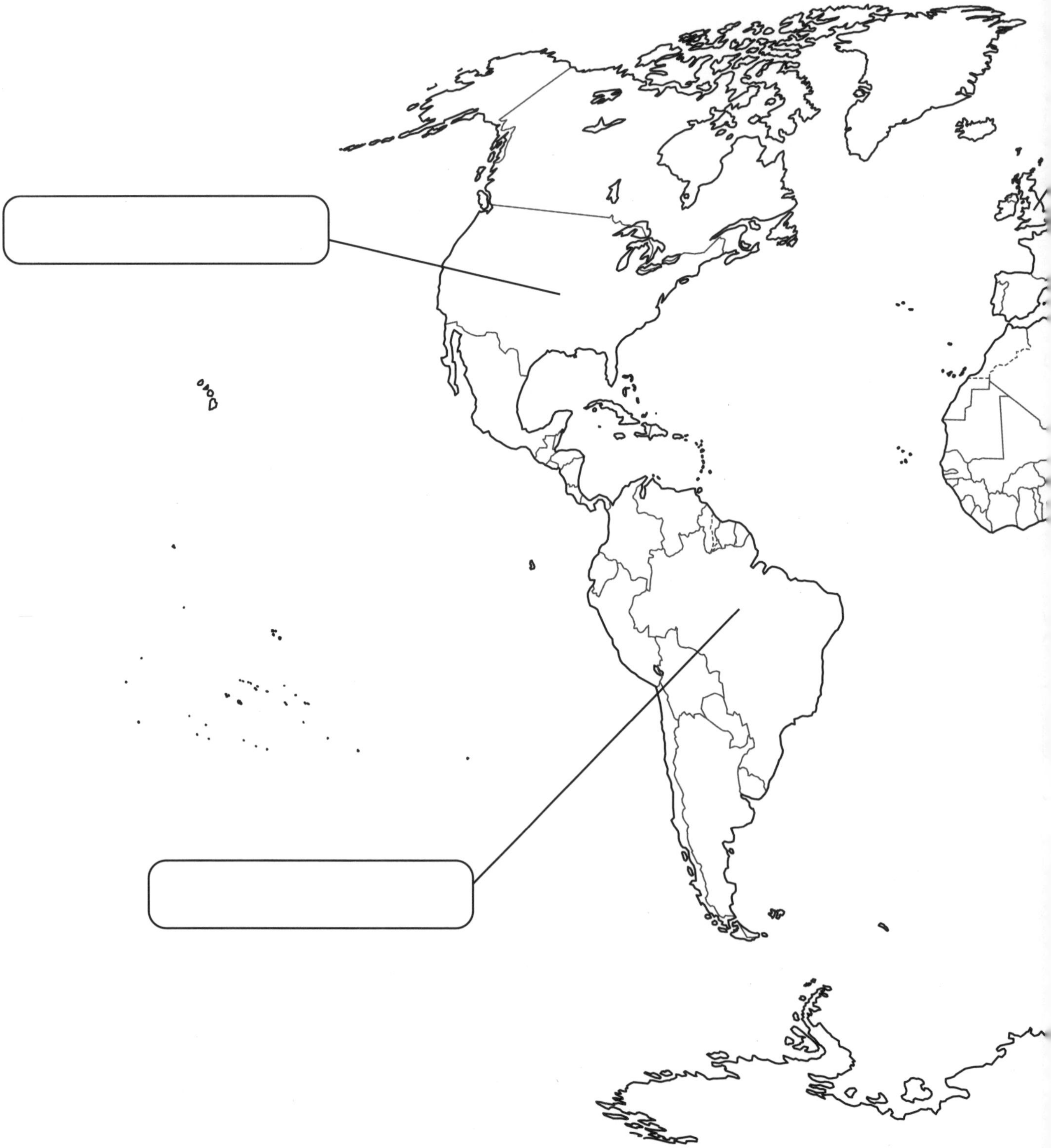

❷ Find your country on the map. Colour it in your favourite colour.
❸ Write one thing that you most love about your country.

> **Hint:** It could be a particular food or the music or a place or person.

_____

_____

_____

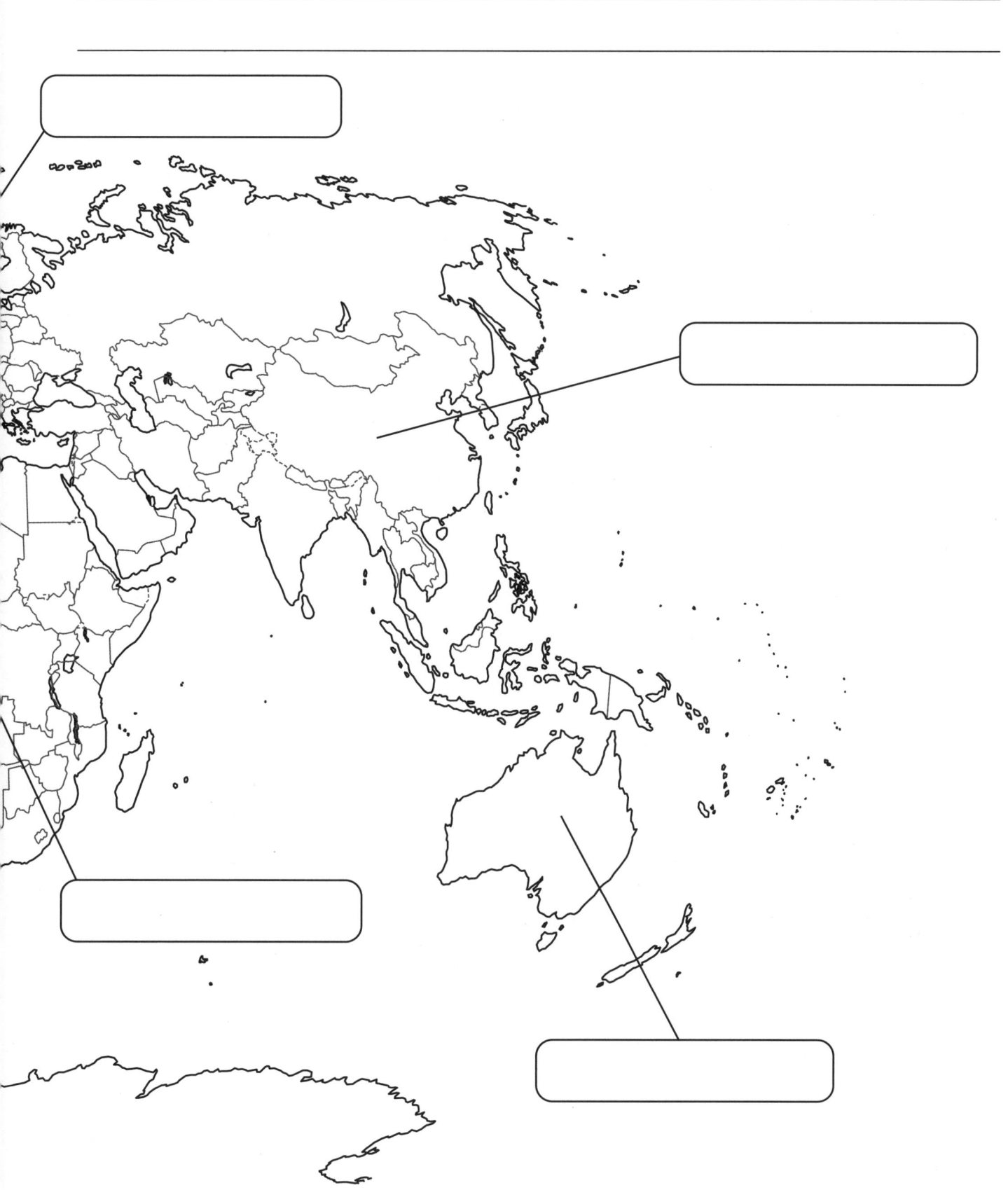

Notes

William Collins' dream of knowledge for all began with the publication of his first book in 1819.

A self-educated mill worker, he not only enriched millions of lives, but also founded a flourishing publishing house. Today, staying true to this spirit, Collins books are packed with inspiration, innovation and practical expertise.

They place you at the centre of a world of possibility and give you exactly what you need to explore it.

Published by Collins
An imprint of HarperCollins*Publishers*
The News Building, 1 London Bridge Street, London, SE1 9GF, UK

HarperCollins*Publishers*
Macken House, 39/40 Mayor Street Upper, Dublin 1, D01 C9W8, Ireland

Browse the complete Collins catalogue at
collins.co.uk

© HarperCollins*Publishers* Limited 2025
Maps © Collins Bartholomew 2025

10 9 8 7 6 5 4 3 2 1

ISBN 978-0-00-872835-9

All rights reserved. No part of this publication may be reproduced, stored in a retrieval system, or transmitted in any form by any means, electronic, mechanical, photocopying, recording or otherwise, without the prior written permission of the Publisher or a licence permitting restricted copying in the United Kingdom issued by the Copyright Licensing Agency Ltd, 5th Floor, Shackleton House, 4 Battle Bridge Lane, London SE1 2HX.

Without limiting the author's and publisher's exclusive rights, any unauthorised use of this publication to train generative artificial intelligence (AI) technologies is expressly prohibited. HarperCollins also exercise their rights under Article 4(3) of the Digital Single Market Directive 2019/790 and expressly reserve this publication from the text and data mining exception.

British Library Cataloguing-in-Publication Data

A catalogue record for this publication is available from the British Library.

Author: Fiona Macgregor
Publisher: Laura White
Product managers: Natasha Paul and Shelley Teasdale
Development editor: Judith Walters
Copyeditor: Fiona Watson
Proofreader: Charlotte Christensen
Cover designer and illustrator: Steve Evans
Internal illustrator: Jouve India Private Ltd
Typesetter: David Jimenez
Production controller: Katie Jean-Baptiste
Printed and bound in the UK by Martins the Printers

This book is produced from independently certified FSC™ paper to ensure responsible forest management.

For more information visit: www.harpercollins.co.uk/green
collins.co.uk/sustainability

Acknowledgements

The publishers gratefully acknowledge the permission granted to reproduce the copyright material in this book. Every effort has been made to trace copyright holders and to obtain their permission for the use of copyright material. The publishers will gladly receive any information enabling them to rectify any error or omission at the first opportunity.

All photos: Shutterstock.